Saying Grace

James P. Lenfestey

Marsh River Editions

Some of these poems were first published, often in earlier versions, in the following publications. Many thanks to the editors for permission to reprint.

Free Verse, The Heartlands Today, Minnesota Monthly, Minnesota Poetry Calendar, 1999

"My Wife Sleeping Beside Me" first appeared in *Proposing on the Brooklyn Bridge: Poems About Marriage,* edited by Ginny Lowe Connors, Grayson Books, 2003.

Thanks to Perry Ingli for cover art.
From the Aerial Panoramic Series:
Farmland View Northeast of River Falls, Wisconsin,
© Ingli July 4, 2000. Pastels on paper.
www.ingliart.com

ISBN 0-9718909-6-X
Publisher/Editor Linda Aschbrenner
Printed by Heinzen Printing Inc., Marshfield, Wisconsin

Marsh River Editions
M233 Marsh Road
Marshfield, WI 54449

For Ted and Jo—

Born in Wisconsin,
bore me in Wisconsin,
taught me to read and write
and swim and drive in Wisconsin,
died in Wisconsin,
bringing me back.
A great love.

Contents

Highway Alphabet

I love to drive the rural highways
in my state named with letters.

To smell fresh-cut alfalfa on A,
sour cheese curds swimming in vats on C,

The burger place on B where cows graze near
the back door not caring what you eat.

Accelerate on D past Drambuie's crumbled shed,
he who steals bellybuttons from lazy boys.

Slow down on Highway P near farmer Gilson's
empty pen of pignapped sows.

Follow S curves through Holstein herds standing still,
barn lights on for early milking.

Take X past the fallen barn and the
rusted pump in the cornfield.

Ease right on Y at the empty quonset,
the gone-to-seed fields giving over to forest.

Weave Z past glimmers of lake resorts
down pine-lined two-tracks.

Such an alphabet thrills city boys
dreaming as we drive,

If only Dad had married the woman who loved horses,
if only we weren't allergic to hay, to loneliness.

Ghost Story, Fourth of July

Say this didn't happen, I swear it did.
Last night in the summer cottage of my youth,
I woke to a bang bang bang outside my window.
Right away I knew it was my father,
dead for thirteen years.
My heart pulled my body into the darkness.
At 3:21 a.m. by the blue glow of the kitchen clock,
I turned toward the waiting door.

It was the wind, big like the old days
when exciting fronts rattled across the bay.
In the neighbor's yard light, trees pitched,
casting vigorous shadows. Whitecaps
formed ghostly lines on black water.
A frayed American flag
waved wildly toward the house.

And I, fat with salty ham, his favorite
food, my belly round like his,
paced for a drink of water, then
back for a drink of wind,
back and forth until birdsong
rang the rim of morning.
Just as he did his last years,
laughing and brooding about the world.

Born and Raised
in Green Bay, Wisconsin:
a Football Autobiography

I put stickum on my hands
in the cold afternoon.

I am surrounded by the steaming breath
of a full house in winter,
a roaring of jackets
pierced by the red eyes
of the networks.

The sun slants low over the end zone
into the eyes of the receivers.
As I jog out onto the frozen field I feel nothing
but the dryness of my hands,
see nothing but the glint off satellites.

This is the last play.
This is the end.

At the temples at Angkor Wat
they pause in the battling and killing
among the water buffalo.

Women in Palo Alto hush on green lawns
among silver platters of crudités, fresh
fruits and cheeses.

African children with inflated bellies look up
wide-eyed from the dirt.

Gang members in Chicago
idle their low cars by the side of the road.

Will it be Green Bay?
Will it be Green Bay?

The quarterback calls the play.
It is the Oedipus at Colonus play.
It is the Gloucester in King Lear play,
the Helen Keller and Ray Charles play.
I won't see the ball. I will have to feel it.

I have studied every aspect of the game—
the trails of hoofed mascots in the frost,
the enormous legs of the four down linemen,
the bright minds wired to headsets.

I will be one-on-one with a cornerback
of great range,
the fastest and cleverest of them all,
a driver of Jaguars.

At the moment of our turning in the end zone,
at the instant of our ascendancy,
I will see only one thing:
the low sun piercing clouds
of silent, held breath.

The quarterback backpedals
over the cracked and bleeding grass.
I turn and leap with my arms
fully extended
and give my body away to the blindness
the way a goose gives its body
to the chopping block.

And whatever happens,
I will feel it first in my fingers.

And the question will be answered.

And the guns and the women and the children
that are silent in wondering
can resume their play.

And I will be carried from the field,
a Green Bay boy
to the end.

At the LCO Powwow

Falsetto songs fall like familiar rain.
Drums pound up under dusty feet.
Dancers follow the sun around,
every return a homecoming.

Near the microphone, a friend laughs.
At the giveaway, another friend receives.
A little money jingles too, and dancers
dignified as bears strut in beaded satin.

And this. Out over the drum arbor
an eagle loped across the sky,
and after a brief, hard rain, a rainbow.
A dream you say, but they joined the dance.

At the LCO powwow, everyone dances—
toddlers, elders, prancing teens and their
thick-set teachers, me, you, rain
and after rain, honoring the earth.

As I drive away from the powwow grounds,
red and white pines reach across the road.

The Origin of Pipestone

One story says the wet finger of God
touched the earth, just here, just there.

Another, that drops of blood fell
from combat among the immortals.

A third tale, the
geologic one,
is no less complicated.

Nanaboujou, Awake!

Nanaboujou sleeps in his island body
outside the harbor at Thunder Bay
below Thunderbird's mountain
downwind from a reeking pulp mill.

You lay down in silence
on your Lake Superior bed
as white men dug
your silver sides.

Now the silver mines are gone,
copper, nickel too.
The electric plant no longer plumes
black smoke for you to breathe
and muskeg woods trap mill waste
once flowing by your side.

Is that not enough?
Will you please awake and save us?
Or can you still not stand the smell?

Requiem for the Iraq National Library

April 13, 2003

Don't you hear the stone lions roaring
and the great bulls bellowing
on the other side of the world?

Ancient Baghdad is burned,
another madness
of school-starved children.

Scrolls of papyrus and the thin skins of sheep
crackle in fire eagerly as rage and ignorance,
flames all scriveners fear.

Praise the three hundred generations
of goutish, near-sighted men
who guarded these flaming scripts.

What heroic vigilance they gave,
holding each tender leaf and skin to the light,
Time's black blood coursing through them.

Now ashes darken the night sky, fluttering
across the sad face of the moon like
swirling migrations of confused bats,

Omens of nothing good arriving
this spring in the world.

A Man in Love with Jackpine

I met a man in love with jackpine.
Built his house from it, heats with it too—
bent, scraggly, rough-scaled, pop-pitched,
up from granite rock through killer snows.

"Live in the north part
of Ontario for two years
and you would love her too," he said.
"That's all there is."

Much more could be said
for having only one choice in love.
Knowing every bitter curve and spit of her.
How strong she is, how hot she burns.

Renaming the Birds

As snow melts into spring buds,
fragrant notes trill like silver drops.
"House finch?" Not the author of that song.

Sing, Flutesong! Trill, Ascender!
Court, Red Stallion, your elusive lovers
flitting in three dimensions!

We drink deeply at the bar of the open,
sun-warmed window. Listening,
not talking, makes us believe.

Playing Tennis at 7 A.M. with a Boy 39 Years My Junior

In the dark, I have no idea
I am too old. My insides,
like a butterfly, feel new.
The streetlight seems right to me,
shedding golden light on pines.

The old dog, dying every day,
manages to bark out his needs.
I carry him to the snowbank
where he struggles to pass toxins
from his body.

When I play the younger man
I win the second game, and three out of nine.
Then two out of eight.
He tells me on the way home how nervous
he was. How he'd like to play again.

In my dream, he marries my daughter—
he taciturn, she giddy.
Something perfect will have been achieved.

The sun turns the few February leaves
into jewels dangling from
the bare arms of winter trees—

Amber, in which lives forever the fully
realized form of fragrant lives.

My Wife Sleeping Beside Me

She trusts no one. Even sleeping
she keeps one foot on the dashboard,
a last defense against troubles.

Without her on watch, the sleeping world
could lose its way, stumble as we
once did into old and painful traps.

The sun sets, rippling the undersides
of clouds with rose and gold.
Her head, heavy on her chest—
rare silhouette—
hushes me at the wheel.

Next to the highway, deer
graze corn stubble in twilight.
At their hooves,
wild turkeys look and feed.

We plunge together our course of earth,
each alert in our own way,
children and grandchildren trailing
behind in radiant plumes,
ahead the blue black sky full
of oncoming lights and stars.

Strawberries

With my children,
I more eager than they,
through the rows,
stooping with joy.

Racing back to the car,
far too many sweet quarts,
berries falling like red pebbles
on the green path.

Driving Across Wisconsin
September 11, 2001

Do the trees know what has happened?
Is that why that one's crown
is rimmed with fire, that one's arm
droops a flagging yellow?

Sumac, thick as people
on a crowded street,
redden suddenly from the tips.

Ferns in dark hollows of the forest
reveal their veins.

Bouquets of asters, purple and white,
offer themselves from the side of the road
to all the wounded passing by.

Saying Grace

Yellow Caterpillars chew day and night
on Highway 29
to save an hour on trips across the state.

That asphalt gift to travelers costs dairy farmers
big in corners cut off fields claimed stone
by stone from glacier till, bound now again
by forces distant, cold, a mile high.

Yet farmers will not leave this place lest sacked
by laws of eminent domain, or hail, or drought,
or a mad king father's razor whip,
or the crush of prices below the cost
to send to cities such delicious ease.

As I race by at sunset late one wet July,
woodlots rake spiked shadows
over fresh-mown fields
where hay bales scatter
in the green like gold doubloons.

Each farm harbors a courtyard
where sacred cattle graze within,
butterflies minuet and ponies joust
and breeze perfumed with hay and sweet manure
breaks waves of wildflowers over the field's edge.

You farmers are the kings, we the shiftless wanderers
in our fast cars wondering at the eminent domain
in which you live. When we say grace,
it is you we praise, your fields so rich and gold
they burn our eyes the way a true king's crown
compels heads down in rank obeisance.

You give us earth groomed easy
for our eyes, abundant on our plates.
In passing, belatedly, I give you thanks.

Roadside Flowers

For Jim Bogan and Will Winter

In the disturbance along the highway
periwinkle blue hands scale their Gaudi stalks,
wild yellow sunbursts ride slender ropes,
a hundred luscious lavenders clump in bowls
while solitary dark threads stiffen under
bursting seedheads of white cotton.

This is where I live.
Not the wild world, woods
cloaked in doeskin and bear scat,
shy with trillium, dead man's
fingers and trout lily.

Nor on the busy line of asphalt climbing the hills.
But at the edge, the space between,
making hearty love out of wasteland.

My colorful friends and I, we are poplar, soft
but swift, first in after fire, leaves flashing.
Blueberries too, tart, big as hatpin heads.
Our birds are buzzard, crow and raven,
our fur coyote.

Not fields plowed in generous rows to feed the multitudes,
corn leaves flopped over like a million elegant scarves.
Nor even the farmer's garden, neat with potatoes.

But vagrants and pioneers, waving wildly
from the side of the road, not even hitch-hiking.
Not doing or making anything but beauty.

Midsummer fuzzy hats of purple fleabane.
Golden-fruited tips of swaying grasses.
Brown bottlebrushes of cattails in low, wet places.
Hillsides mounded yellow with puccoon.
The spindly pale architecture of chicory.
A swath of black-eyed Susans engulfing
a fallen fence.

What the Soul Looks Like

As a boy, I sat
in hard-backed pews.
Every week, the word
was spoken.

I imagined it
fitted into my chest,
a cross like the medical staff
on my grandfather's stationery,
wrapped with snakes
and flowers.

For forty years I've wondered,
is that the soul?
The doctor's hand that let me go
as he fell away to die?
My father's car that rolled away
without a driver?

Open Casket

Pulled by my father's firm grip,
I peered up over the rim. There lay
someone gray, sunken, pillowed in silk,
said to be my grandfather.
The hand that held me
pulsed like a heartbeat.

When my father died, my mother, sisters and I
too threw open the casket door.
We sprayed rouge on his cheeks
and forehead, he looked so pale.
I reached to smooth an errant sleeve,
a touch I never dared at four,
and found out why.

That hand that held me, hot and wet
when I knew nothing of what loss meant,
was cold as ice.
My fingers burn still with that sharp lesson,
like knuckles rapped by a stern teacher.

Death's door opens not in but out
an open casket toward hot, wet
hands surrounding it in grief,
buried sometimes for decades
before dug up, fresh and warm
as delicate spring blossoms.

Old Songs

(for JFB, DduPW and JBI)

When you are dying, only ripples
remain—old songs sung when you
were young as now, lying soft
and cradled on the watery shore.

Rhymes, creeds, show tunes,
Negro spirituals, poems
droned by Mother Goose, high
priests and high school teachers,

Boomed by your father
on long cold nights, crooned
by your mother as you fell asleep,
flow from you now near water

Where the rhythm of waves
is louder than the rhythm of wind and violins.
Waves that lap the same low shore where you
washed up, gasping, startled to be alive,

Thirsty still for the waters behind you,
liquid that filled your swelling lungs
with an old song you are remembering now,
will soon sing once more.

Passing a Sign to the Central Wisconsin Town of Jim Falls

Hey, that's my name, and state—
descended from undistinguished King James,
obsolete as his office,
memorable only for his translators' tongue.

Yea, though I drive through this valley
without shadows
on the longest day of summer,
Jim falls, has fallen, oh how very far.

I can only pray the cliff in this quilted landscape
of modest hills and modest people
over which my tongues of poems pour
is high, at least, as an average man.

So there is at least some reflection, some pause
before the tumble at the lip,
the pitch, the flight,
the inevitable, ironic applause.

Dead Deer with Flies

Roadside shimmer.
Bloated white belly.
Black orbiting moons.

The Day I Was Shamed
by Two Amish

Speeding in the car two hundred miles
toward my dying mother,
my wife speeding back the other way,
I saw two bicyclists riding side by side.

I noted quickly the black cross
of suspenders, the sunbonnet,
the gingham billowing over the ankle,
their upright stance.

As they shrank to nothing in my rear-view mirror,
I felt ashamed
by their easy conversation at day's end,
the green crops of June
spread around them like a comforter.

The best we can give each other
at eternal moments
is what they seem to give so easily
across a bicycle on a summer's day,
companionship
surrounded by a shared world
they do not feel the need
to fully own or understand.

The Invitation

Deer abound, living and slaughtered,
along the highways of my state,
coursing the earth as recklessly as sons
who drive too fast in dying light

Toward Mother's dying next to hayfields
that God and farmer Gilson worked
since his mother in her sunbonnet
put up the hay in armload shocks.

They guard the field for you, protect
its swale, its mists, its abundant
birds attending now in conspicuous gold
and black to your feeder,

Like me, eager to display where they
have traveled,
not knowing, like you at ninety-five,
where we travel to.

II

I cross the Wolf River in the dark,
recognizing its smell and angle of descent,
a marker that I am nearing home
as an owl startles the high beams' edge.

Nothing else familiar. Only anonymous eyes
of souls liberating themselves left and right
from the gravity of life before the moon comes up.

This darkness marked by wolves and owls
has never felt so moist, its roots tangled
in moss and loam. Down there the tree
holds its ball of earth as large, larger
than the crown above.

III

The green waters of the bay, smoldering
with weeds, pull me on,
past where my father stands in a roadside park
like a bronze explorer
waiting for us in the sweet-smelling dark.

I am greeted on arrival by a billion stars
and the gold illumination of your tired lamp,
the dark space between finally large enough
for the soul to accept its open invitation.

Getting Close to Home

I swear that woman passing me in the silver
Grand Am is Betty Larsen, though
she's been dead ten years or more,
and wouldn't be caught dead
in a Grand Am.
But that's her platinum bouffant hairdo,
her profile straining forward to get home
before her husband
to greet Don at the door in
fresh makeup, fresh lipstick,
a fresh drink in her hand
for his hard day.

And that man riding the Harley next to me—
that generous belly under the strap
T-shirt, the thin arms,
the wispy white hair blowing
from under the kerchief—
that man is my father,
who never rode a Harley,
only horses.

I must be close to home.

The Red Ant

A red ant forages the Subaru's dashboard
seeking familiar scented trails,
unaware he's uprooted
with a roadside bouquet.

We drive together eighty miles
to reservation woods
as thick with bears as people

To grieve an Indian friend's mother
who lived long enough
to have four daughters forgive.

The red ant rides in my universe
as I in theirs, all in another we do not see,
but feel sometimes, faintly,

In a rhythm rumbling deep below,
or in airy whispers through the trees,
indicating, I believe,
the sea.

Crossing the Freeway

It's November, hunting season.
I could see you clearly in the
golden early morning light
bursting through cut cornstalks
in a fatal dusting of fresh snow.

Behind me, an armada of semis.
Before me, you, beauty, racing toward me
in full stride across the median.

Doubt will kill us now.
Slow down? Swerve? Hesitate?
Turn back in panic toward the median?

Hope lies only through me,
lone driver tapping the brakes
from seventy-five.

As you glide by my nose,
white clouds trail
from your straining nostrils
until you gain the margin of the woods.

Life thrills
at encounters like this—
choices to make,
then the race forward at full speed.

Signs of failure are everywhere.
Every few miles
red entrails spray the center line,
bloated bellies float in shoulder weeds,
crows pick at crumpled hide and bones,
white tails flag the passing wind.

And between those bloody markers?
Ten thousand invisible successes—
swift, decisive contrails melting
into the soft, nibbling bark
of next year's wobbly fawns.

In Josephine's Garden

The tulips come up in regulation rows
in Josephine's garden,
after the daffodils, before
the heavy peonies oozing with ants.

Here we are invited to grow
green and bright-colored,
with beauty before us.

Here we sing the sunsets down—
her alto harmonizing streaks of gold
with blossoms lighting up the ground.

In Josephine's garden, sunsets sing
in the bright company of flowers—
never dull, never old,
only beauty before us.

What Am I Doing
in Paradise, Michigan?

What am I doing now that I'm in Paradise?
Writing poems.
What was I doing before, in the busy world?
Writing poems, when I wasn't too busy.
What will I do when I and my poems are dust?
Do you see the wind riffling the waters of the lake?
Do you hear the moan in that white pine?

James P. Lenfestey is a poet and writer living in Minnesota and Michigan. He has worked as a college literature instructor, director of an alternative school, marketing communications consultant to high tech companies, playwright, and editorial writer at the Minneapolis *StarTribune* where he won several Page One awards.

At Metropolitan State University, he taught American Indian Literature and The Literature of Comedy. He performed a one-man show at The Mixed Blood Theatre and authored, with artistic director Jon Cranney, *Coyote Discovers America*, which premiered the 25th season of The Children's Theatre Company of Minneapolis.

He has published eleven chapbooks of poems, including *Affection for Spiders* (Red Dragonfly Press, 2004) and a collection of personal essays, *The Urban Coyote: Howlings on Family, Community and the Search for Peace and Quiet* (Nodin Press, 2000).

SAYING GRACE

by James P. Lenfestey
was printed in an edition of 400 copies.
It is the seventh publication of Marsh River Editions.
Series design by Nicholas Aschbrenner.